LET OUR CHILDREN LEARN

Allowing ownership
Providing support
Celebrating achievement

Tony Brown   Michael Foot
Peter Holt

With a Foreword
by
Professor Tim Brighouse

Education Now Books

Published 2001 by Education Now Publishing Co-operative Ltd.
113 Arundel Drive, Bramcote Hills, Nottingham NG9 3FQ
in partnership with

Copyright © 2001 Michael Foot, Tony Brown and Peter Holt

British Cataloguing in Publication Data

Foot, Michael,
       Let our children learn: allowing ownership, providing
       support, celebrating achievement
       1. Education – Philosophy 2. Education – Aims and
       Objectives 3. Learning, Psychology of 4. Education –
       Experimental methods – Case studies
I. Title II Brown, Tony III. Holt, Peter
370.1

ISBN 1-871526-49-3

Design and production: Education Now with the authors

Printed by Mastaprint, Ltd., Sandiacre, Nottingham

We dedicate this book to Class 3 of Wimbotsham County Primary School, and to children and their parents and teachers everywhere.

THANK YOU

To Annette, Wendy and Julia, for their classroom presence and assistance over the two days.

To those other schools in which we have recently worked, for unfailingly demonstrating the potential of children and adults to achieve way beyond the constraints now imposed by national educational policy:
Fordham C. of E. Primary School, Cambridgeshire.
Guillemont County Junior School, Cove, Hampshire.
Mundesley County Junior School, Norfolk.
Runcton Holme C. of E. Primary School, Norfolk.
Tuckswood County First School, Norwich, Norfolk.
Wiggenhall St. Mary Magdalen County Primary School, Norfolk.

To Tina and Paul Berry, Peter Durrant, Helen Porter and Lady Rose Hare, for reading and commenting upon a draft text of our book.

To Catherine Brown and Martin Rooke, for their skill and effort in amalgamating typescripts and copying artwork.

To Caroline Ridsdill at the Downham Business Technology Centre, for her unfailingly cheerful and skilled guidance, and for taking us, via (for us!) daunting technology, from first-draft manuscript to ready copy over very many patient weeks.

To Barbara Brown, for countless wonderful working lunches.

To Professor Tim Brighouse, for providing an inimitable Foreword.

To Professor Roland Meighan and Janet Meighan of *Education Now* for their belief in our work.

We are very grateful to you all. In your various ways you have encouraged and supported us so willingly.

THANK YOU

LET OUR CHILDREN LEARN

CONTENTS
(The illustrations are italicised)

FOREWORD

One of our great educators, Sir Alec Clegg, the Chief Education Officer of the West Riding, in the golden quarter century that followed the 1944 Education Act, coined the phrase 'hyacinths and loaves'. He was inspired by a folk poem on his aunt's wall which argued that if you only had two pennies you would buy a loaf of bread with one and a bunch of hyacinths with the other – the first to feed the stomach, the second your spirit and soul.

He went on to argue that there were parts of the curriculum which were loaves and other parts hyacinths. The learning, or study, of a piece of Shakespeare – even its performance – would be the equivalent of a loaf. But the improvised performance by a group or an individual – or even a particular rendition – might be a hyacinth. The notion informs me still. I divide my diary into time of hyacinths – for me conversation and observation in visits to schools – in order that I can service the diet of loaves.

Maybe Sir Alec did not mean that, but that is how I have interpreted what he wrote in his book *'About Our Schools'*. Put another way, it is about creating on the one hand and using it up on the other; and it is about needing to replenish the well of intellectual curiosity without which little is achieved in the school room or the school system.

This book is about hyacinths and the creation of energy. It is written by unquiet spirits whose voices are like dogs barking in the night, but whose message does more than telegraph hidden danger – indeed (mixing metaphors) provides a voice of hope in a world full of confused messages.

You will enjoy reading the book and allowing the reality of schools and the joyful unpredictability of learning and ideas to wash over you.

The work has been put together by people who are 'driven' in the best sense of the word. Like all good teachers they are generous and I thank them for their generosity in writing the book.

Professor Tim Brighouse
Chief Education Officer
Birmingham LEA

Magical feather give me flight   (Edward)

Chapter 1

THE REALMS OF GOLD

"Much have I travell'd in the realms of gold,"
(Keats: 'On First Looking into Chapman's Homer')

"It is, in fact, nothing short of a miracle that the modern methods of instruction have not yet entirely strangled the holy curiosity of enquiry; for this delicate little plant, aside from stimulation, stands mainly in need of freedom; without this it goes to rack and ruin without fail. It is a very grave mistake to think that the enjoyment of seeing and searching can be promoted by means of coercion and a sense of duty." (Albert Einstein)

We would like to tell you a story. It is a story with a beginning, but we believe it has no end. It is a true story.

To the extent that language is ever able to be a camera, and montage is ever able to create and communicate a whole picture, you will see as accurate a portrait as we can manage of the events which make up this story. In addition, we have marbled the portrait, throughout its length, with quotations. Most of these we glory in; some take us to the edge of despair.

Once upon a time, a group of children and a group of adults came together for a couple of days, and travelled a journey. In truth, we had all travelled a journey *in the process of becoming what we were at the start of Day One* – all of us, particularly we adults, but that's another story, for another time.

We adults had first announced ourselves, and our purpose, through a letter. (See Appendix C.) The children each received one, outlining the plan for the two days in general terms, and explaining who the visiting adults would be. Three of us were already known to them in fact, so it was the fourth name which was completely new. A retired Senior County Adviser and three retired primary Headteachers might sound a little formidable in some quarters, but to the children that group simply represented a clutch of fresh faces. The children were all alert to the prospect of a new experience; for our part, we were about to set foot on a journey of faith.

Bring in a natural object. Sketch it. Paint it. Research it. Write creatively about it. Put those four pieces of work into a book of your own making.

There. Quite straightforward. But *two days?* Two whole days!

Before describing that two-day journey on the trail of a book, we have some chapters of background information for you.

> *"We should wake up to what's happening. Setting is part of a tranche of changes in state primary education which, together, are putting unacceptable pressures on children too young to understand or negotiate them. First there were the Standard Attainment Tests, (SATs); then the school league tables; now there's base line assessment, treated by many as 'exams for five year olds' ...Setting is just the final phase in creating a formidable culture of success and failure in our primary schools. With their emphasis on bringing out the best in all pupils in mixed ability classes in the past these schools have been a powerful force for social integration. Now all of that is being destroyed in order to pander to Woodhead's obsessions and save Blunkett's career...The only way of ensuring the best education for all children is by training and supporting good teachers – not by dumping harmful anxiety and competitiveness on little children."*
> *(Ros Coward. 'Suffering in Year Six'. The Guardian, 19th January 1999)*

> *"The number of children experiencing mental ill health has increased since the 1940s to an estimated one in five. Mental health problems in children and young people will continue to increase unless there is a coherent and holistic programme implemented to develop the emotional and mental health of our children and to intervene early when problems do develop...*

4

Schools have a critical role to play in creating emotionally literate children and in the early identification and referral of children with mental health problems. The current pressures on schools, for example the demands of the National Curriculum, are making it more difficult for schools to attend to promoting the needs of the whole child."
('The Big Picture – Promoting children and young people's mental health': The Mental Health Foundation, 1999)

Chapter 2

THE VILLAGE

"Here, where the world is quiet."
(A. C. Swinburne: 'The Garden Of Prosperine')

Wimbotsham is unremarkable.

Nothing of note appears to have happened since Winebald the Anglo-Saxon established his homestead there nearly a millennium and a half ago.

No battle of Civil or any other war is recorded as having been fought there; no building boasts a blue plaque to tell that anybody who achieved other than local fame or notoriety was born, or lived, or died there; the war memorial celebrates much heroism, but such lists of deceased heroes are, sadly, the commonplace of English villages; there is no magnificent architecture or scenic beauty to warrant its inclusion on many tourist itineraries. Even its 1960s 'love-in' attracted only three hundred flower power enthusiasts, rather than the thousands that the locals had expected and feared.

So, neither in Defoe's *'Tour Through The Whole Island Of Great Britain'*, nor in Cobbett's *'Rural Rides'*, nor even in Bill Bryson's *'Notes From A Small Island'*, does Winebald's homestead merit a mention.

It is situated just a mile or so north of the town of Downham Market in West Norfolk. It is by-passed by the main A10 road; this road connects with the market town of King's Lynn about ten miles to the north and with Ely and beyond to the south.

At first I thought it was a mineral called Beryl because it had the same sort of green and the same sort of crystally look to it.

6

But then I found out that you could only find Beryl in Brazil, Colombia, India, Madagascar, Namibia, Pakistan, South Africa, Zimbabwe.

But I found mine in Kent!!!
(Kelly B)

There is a Church of England church, a Methodist chapel, a surprisingly large village store with post office, and a triangular village green which was memorably described in her poem a couple of years ago by one of the children of the village school as a place

where daisies chime and dandelions ring.

On one each of the three sides of the village green stand the elderly village hall, the welcoming 'Chequers' public house, and Wimbotsham County Primary School.

"A sleepy world of streams"
(A. C. Swinburne: 'The Garden Of Prosperine')

Quartz   (Danny)

Chapter 3

THE SCHOOL

"Education is not concerned only with equipping students with the knowledge and skills they need to earn a living. It must help our young people: to use leisure time creatively; have respect for other people, other cultures and other beliefs; become good citizens; think things out for themselves; pursue a healthy life-style; and, not least, value themselves and their achievements. It should develop an appreciation of the richness of our cultural heritage and of the spiritual and moral dimensions to life. It must, moreover, be concerned to serve all our children well, whatever their background, sex, creed, ethnicity or talent."

(Para.3.11 of Ron Dearing's final report on 'The National Curriculum and its Assessment', December 1993)

At the time of our visit Wimbotsham School had 82 pupils on roll, aged between 4 and 11 years. This represented a significant growth in pupil numbers from around 50 and falling about eight years earlier. This growth is indicative of the higher esteem in which the school is now held by its local and wider community.

As well as its home village, the school serves the neighbouring village of Stowbridge where the small primary school was closed in 1989. Also attending Wimbotsham School are children living in two other neighbouring villages, Stow Bardolph and Runcton Holme, and a few who travel from Downham Market and King's Lynn.

The old school building dates from 1869 and 1894. In 1995 an extension was built comprising two classrooms, staffroom and office, and indoor toilets. The old school building was remodelled so that it now contains just one classroom (the lower infant room), school hall and a kitchen servery. The school has an area of hard playground, an adventure playground which is the result of a self-help project, a small grassed play area, and a garden which is cultivated by the children and which is the result of another self-help initiative. The children also have use of the adjacent and large village recreation ground for some sporting purposes.

> *"Education must be based on the view that all persons are created equal and that human dignity is inviolable. It should confirm the belief that everyone is unique; that each can nourish his own growth and that individual distinctions enrich and enliven our world."*
> *('Core Curriculum for Primary, Secondary and Adult Education in Norway', 1994)*

In November 1998, very shortly after our two days working in the school, Mr. Chris Woodhead, the then Chief Inspector of Schools, visited at the invitation of the school. He was invited so that he might see at first hand something of the school's achievements and so that some members of the school's teaching staff and governing body who were available could share with him their concerns about a number of recent and current national educational developments.

To coincide with his visit, the mother of a Wimbotsham pupil wrote to Mr Woodhead. She told him of her especial anxieties about national curriculum assessment of children and about performance tables for their schools. From its very first word her letter says much about the sense of belonging within its community which the school enjoys. It goes on to show a massive understanding of the school's values and purposes and it displays a commendable desire to describe those values and purposes to the Chief Inspector as the context for her concerns. It reads, in part:

> *"Our school attempts to create an ethos, an atmosphere that encourages our children to be confident, caring individuals with a drive and enthusiasm to search out knowledge and enjoy it. I could find no grading that reflected this in my daughter's results or in our school's position in the league."*

The school's 82 pupils were shared between three classes. The lower infant class of 27 pupils included children of national curriculum years R and 1. The upper infant/lower junior class of 27 pupils included children of years 2, 3 and 4.

We worked with Class 3, the upper junior class of 28 children of years 4, 5 and 6 whose class teacher was the head teacher.

10

"Dear Teacher,

I am the survivor of a concentration camp. My eyes saw what no man should witness:

Gas chambers built by learned engineers; children poisoned by educated physicians; infants killed by trained nurses; women and babies shot and burned by high school and college graduates;

So I am suspicious of education.

My request is, help your students become human.

Your efforts must never produce learned monsters, skilled psychopaths, educated Eichmanns.

Reading, writing and arithmetic are important only if they serve to make our children more human."

Yes! Yes! Yes!

Chapter 4

THE CLASS

"It is important that students bring a certain ragamuffin, barefoot irreverence to their studies; they are not here to worship what is known, but to question it."
(Jacob Bronowski)

There were 14 girls, 14 boys, 28 in total – 13 of them in national curriculum year 6, 11 of them in year 5, 4 of them in year 4; having said which – 28 children!

It is their individuality which the school chooses to celebrate, properly preferring to recognise and to try to accommodate that individuality rather than pretending, for example, that just because a child is of a particular age there is a set of similar academic expectations which can be made of that child and all of his/her peers. So, for we visitors working with this mixed age and (like all classes!) mixed ability class, there was no sense of knowing or of needing to know which were the older and which were the younger children. In educational rather than organisational terms, one of the least important things that we (or anybody) should need to know about any child is that child's age.

The class was used to making choices, to exercising self-discipline, and thus to acting responsibly; indeed the way in which we worked with the children would not have been possible without this background. As with other aspects of their development, people generally get better at making choices and at exercising self-discipline if they have frequent opportunities to practise doing so. Responsibility is not generally a quality which suddenly appears, without preparation, in late teens. No. It is something which will be the result of a childhood which allows the practice of responsibility so that it can continue and develop into adulthood.

So, and as one example of this, we heard no bells or whistles. We saw no simmering lines of children stretched into the playground from the school door, awaiting a teacher's permission for them to enter. Instead, at the appropriate times the children entered the school in ones and fews at the invitation of the teacher on duty or on seeing their classmates already doing so.

Despite the enormous pressures which all schools currently experience to narrow the curriculum so as to emphasise literacy and numeracy and thus to marginalise other vital areas, Wimbotsham School legitimately continues to see curriculum entitlement in terms of the broad and the balanced; it continues to see literacy and numeracy as part of a wider and richer whole; indeed it continues to see the development of literacy and numeracy as being best served within that wider and richer context.

For these reasons, in the same term as our visit, the children worked for a day with a London-based artist of international repute; they welcomed five members of the English Shakespeare Company for a workshop performance of *'Twelfth Night'*; and the school did not, like some schools, cancel their Christmas concerts 'because of the literacy hour'!

> *The seahorse is a strange animal which lives in the sea. All seahorses*
> *are prickly and can sometimes hurt if you press on them too hard.*
>
> *The bit on the back is called the dorsal fin. The tail of a seahorse is*
> *like a monkey's tail. It is called a prehensile tail.*
>
> *Seahorses usually swim around a seaweed called orange sea-whip, it*
> *is a very strange name for some seaweed.*
>
> *The most strangest thing in the whole wide world, the male seahorse*
> *has a baby. The female lays the eggs inside the male and the male has*
> *a sort of pouch which the baby seahorses come out of.*
> *(Michael)*

The school's celebration of individual differences is further evidenced by the decision not to impose a school uniform upon the children, a temptation to which so many primary schools have now succumbed. Do these schools really believe that school uniform somehow promotes the *'spiritual, moral, cultural, mental and physical development'* of their pupils? Do they really believe that it assists in the preparation for responsible adulthood? At Wimbotsham School the children can make guided choices in dressing appropriately for school.

It was the richness of their school experience, the celebration of their differences, their willingness and practised ability to make choices and to exercise self-discipline, and their consequent enthusiasm for learning, which together made possible all that the children achieved during our time with them.

"At the same time I was seeing more and more evidence that most adults actively distrust and dislike most children..."
(John Holt)

"Most adults in fact speak as though they have never been children."
('The Big Picture – Promoting children and young people's mental health': The Mental Health Foundation, 1999)

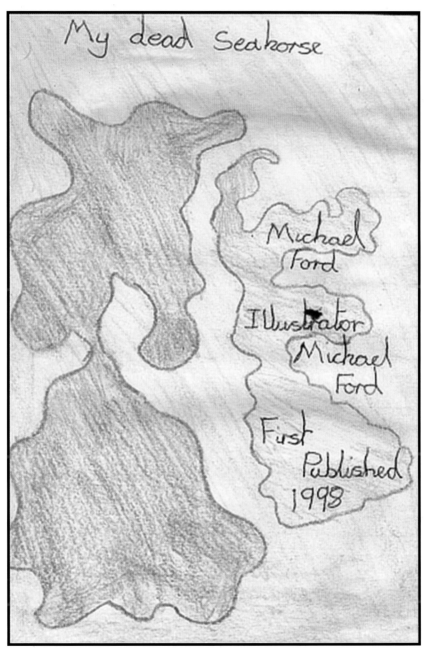

Seahorse: **The most strangest thing in the whole wide world...** (Michael)

Chapter 5

THE CHILD

> *"At the heart of the educational process lies the child..."*
> *('Children and their Primary Schools', the Plowden Report, 1967)*

Yet now we read the claim that:

> *"At the centre of the learning process are the texts..."*
> *(Bill Tindall, literacy consultant, writing in 'New Childhood', Winter 1998/1999, the journal of the National Association for Primary Education)*

A class of 28 individuals in a school of 82 children. So why choose Joanne to write about?

The answer is to do with her very special achievements and with her vulnerability – and with these things within a national context which increasingly judges and compares on the basis of a narrow and narrowing range of achievement. Her very specialness - and that of children like her all over the country - serves to illustrate and to emphasise the dangerously misguided nature of much recent and current policy-making. It also serves to illustrate faith being rewarded.

Joanne had arrived new to school as a troubled and aggressive soul. She was in many respects less mature and less able than most of her peers, and she came with the dubious distinction of having been expelled from the pre-school play-bus. In consequence of all of this, Joanne was not popular with her classmates, various of whom would retire home at the end of the school day nursing the bitten and bruised evidence of her physical attentions.

Nearly five years on, Joanne, still hampered by academic difficulties, is at peace with herself and with her world. Joanne has flowered; she has flowered within and because of a school ethos which prefers to emphasise co-operation rather than competition, which celebrates achievements in all fields and at all levels, which regards parents as vital players in their children's education, and which believes all of its children to be of equal worth.

> "As the old man walked along the beach at dawn, he noticed a young man ahead of him picking up starfish and flinging them into the sea.
>
> Finally catching up with the youth, he asked him why he was doing this. The answer was that the stranded starfish would die if left until the morning sun.
>
> 'But the beach goes on for miles and there are millions of starfish,' countered the other. 'How can your effort make a difference?'
>
> The young man looked at the starfish in his hand and then threw it to safety in the waves. 'It makes a difference to this one,' he said."
> (Minnesota Literacy Council)

Earlier in the year, on the school's five-day residential visit to Holt Hall in North Norfolk, Joanne famously inspired in an adult a poem with her inimitable observation as she and he crossed the Hall's grounds on a golden, still, winter's morning: *"The trees i 'n 't gristling in the wind."* The poem came to be included in Holt Hall's new brochure and so Joanne's words reached into all of the schools in Norfolk and many beyond. Joanne the poet; Joanne the inspiration for others. (See Appendix E.)

At one point during our two days together, Joanne was close by when Michael was considering a draft of his poem about his seahorse. *"It's better without the it's"* was Joanne's judgement – a judgement agreed to by Michael. Joanne the poet; Joanne, at peace with herself, the inspiration for others. Thus, the final version of Michael's poem appeared:

I HAVE A SEAHORSE

I have a seahorse
A seahorse it is
Spiky and prickly
Like squeezing a thorn bush.

16

I have a seahorse
A seahorse it is
Brown and strange
How does it live?

I have a seahorse
A seahorse it is
Mouth like a hoover
Sucking its dinner.
(Michael)

Joanne is innocent enough at a recent Christmas to have declaimed with massive integrity about the nativity model which stood in the school's entrance hall: *"Don't that farmyard look lovely"*, and for her directness to be respected by the nearby children and adult when doing so.

And yet her gradually and hard-won confidence and her peace of mind are, we fear, fragile things which are at risk, because Joanne and those like her, whatever their enormous achievements, will always be in the underachieving corner of the statisticians' scattergraphs, will always feature in the underachieving column of their bar charts.

For Joanne's enormous achievements transcend the simplistic measures and the arrogant certainties of those who would judge and compare children and schools, and then publish their results as if holy scripture.

When Joanne and the dozen or so others in her year group engage in their key stage 2 assessment, she will represent about 8% of her school's aggregated score. Joanne's teachers and her school risk denigration from those who choose to invest school performance/league tables with a validity which they do not merit. The 'Joannes' of this fiercely competitive educational world risk becoming liabilities who militate against their schools' higher standing.

Significantly, it was first the presence and then the absence of a couple of 'Joannes' which caused Wimbotsham School's position in the published league table of West Norfolk primary schools to veer from one year to the next from 130-something to 30-something. And lamentably, the school's local Member of Parliament who wrote to congratulate the school on its improved position was none other than the then Secretary of State for Education – who really ought to have

17

known better and whose misguided simplicities of belief and policy put at risk Joanne, her like, and their schools.

Thankfully, for now and for the time being Joanne is in the sympathetic and understanding hands of people who recognise and value and celebrate her very substantial attributes and achievements. But we are bound to be concerned for her longer-term future, for the continuing recognition of her attributes and achievements, for her happiness, in an educational environment which – unless there is a major change of national direction – seems bound to focus upon her shortcomings rather than her strengths.

Joanne enjoyed her two days. She drew and painted, researched and wrote, and made her book. She advised and was advised. And her achievements were very properly celebrated.

> *"Many people are handicapped in relation to their surroundings. Education must confer knowledge about, and foster equal worth and solidarity for those whose skills differ from those of the majority. And, not least, it should promote the appreciation that any one of us can be struck by illness or injury, by destitution, tribulations, or anguish, all of which can make us dependent on the compassion of others."*
> *('Core Curriculum for Primary, Secondary and Adult Education in Norway', 1994)*

Yes! Yes! Yes!

Fossil: Joanne's enormous achievements transcend the simplistic measures and the arrogant certainties of those who would judge and compare children and schools...

Chapter 6

THE PLANNING

"The central factor emerging from this study is that a degree of teacher direction is necessary, and that this direction needs to be carefully planned."
(Neville Bennett: 'Teaching Styles And Pupil Progress')

A journey should be planned, sort of!

It is not that the leaders want to predict, or indeed are foolish enough to think that they can predict, every step on the way. No. It is just that, having decided to set out, then some time frame, some vital equipment, some sort of leadership roles, must be decided upon, otherwise the party simply becomes a loose, wandering, aimless lot, and people become vulnerable.

So we planned.

As explained in our opening chapter, *'The Realms of Gold'*, we would ask every child to bring to school a natural object which they would study. Each natural object would be one person's choice from all of the vast array of possibilities; each would be different from all of the others; each would be the particular focus of study of only one person. A sense of ownership – of object and of study – should develop.

There would be many other choices for the children to make – in tools and materials, in working areas, in the order of tackling tasks, in which colours to mix, in which words to use…

We would recommend that the children do their art work before their writing because we believe that the latter is facilitated by and is enhanced by the close

19

observation which the drawing and the painting require. Too often have we and other teachers invited children to draw a picture after they have finished their writing – art as a time filler!

It was at this time that we agreed to write a letter to each of the children to introduce them to the two days. (See Appendix C.)

We agreed that every child would make a book in which, along with a title page and an 'about the author' page, there would be a pencil drawing and a painting of their object; a piece of research writing about their object; and a piece of their own original writing, perhaps in the form of a poem. But beyond this, all things would be possible – and most would be welcomed!

We talked a lot about the form of the beginning and the end of sessions and decided that, apart from the first introductory session, we would hope to allow sessions to begin without a whole-class briefing. Thus the children, when returning to their classroom, would be explicitly returning to their tasks. All sessions would end with some sort of plenary.

We discussed our various potential roles and those of the other adults whom we expected to be available. We considered the pros and cons of working spaces, how to make best use of the classroom space as well as the possible use of spaces outside the classroom – corridor, school office, staffroom, school library.

We agreed the importance of ensuring that books, tools and materials were readily available for the children. All of the necessary papers in an appropriate range of colours and sizes would be prepared in advance of our two days with the children and would then be clearly labelled and made available in their classroom.

> *I think that this fossil was found at Crimplesham gravel pit about 25 years ago.*
>
> *Fossils are hardened remains of animals that lived many millions of years ago. They can be teeth, bones or sometimes all the animal!*
>
> *Lots of fossils are found where the sea is or was. The creature died, the body sank into the seabed. The flesh bits rotted away, the skeleton became buried in the mud.*
>
> *About 570 million years ago mud settled on the top of the skeleton. It eventually turned to rock, the skeleton became part of the rock. The*

water that creeps in the rock slowly dissolved away the original skeleton. It was replaced by stony minerals which formed exactly the same shape.

The oldest known fossil is over three billion years old!
(Clare)

We would require the children to treat all tools and materials with a proper respect, to use the most appropriate tools and materials for any given task, and to leave them ready for use by others when finished with. By this sort of 'best craftsman's' attitude the children would be able to make the most of the opportunity to be independent learners. We recognised classroom organisation as an area of central importance and one which has considerable implications for ways of working and learning, although we do fear that generally these implications are insufficiently recognised and thus classroom organisation is too often neglected.

We agreed that we would emphasise quality in the children's work, with a recognition that quality nearly always requires time as well as care and endeavour. So, if necessary the children could have more time to complete their work after our two days with them.

In our experience, too many people are too concerned with what they call 'the pace of lessons'. We would ensure that unrealistic demands of time would not be made of the children as artists, as writers, as researchers, as craftsmen…as learners. Indeed we find it salutary for ourselves on occasions to be artists, writers, researchers, craftsmen…learners. We commend the experience to all who would require children to be so.

> *"They (teachers) are more than the technicians which many fear the 'teaching by numbers' approach of the national curriculum might encourage; they have at their fingertips a range of complex classroom skills based on a theoretical underpinning as vital as that of any other profession."*
> *(Professor Tim Brighouse. The Observer, 14th March 1993)*

We planned for a journey which would be enjoyed; a journey where to rush would be to risk missing some of the best scenery; a journey to be savoured; a journey to be lingered over; a journey where the occasional rest *en route* would be encouraged; a journey to be talked about; a journey to be remembered.

21

"Education must therefore be structured in such a way that the learners themselves can take part in the further development of inherited practices and in the acquisition of new knowledge."
('Core Curriculum for Primary, Secondary and Adult Education in Norway', 1994)

Chapter 7

THE MAKING OF BOOKS

"Spoon feeding in the long run teaches us nothing but the shape of the spoon."
(E. M. Forster)

At the outset, and to our great delight, Max decided to go beyond our suggestion that the children should begin with a sketch or a painting of their object.

Max decided to make a *rubbing* of his object – a piece of bark. He followed up his rubbing with no fewer than three sketches. Those were *his* considered decisions. He had established a powerful claim to the ownership of his learning. Is this important?

Consider the vast amount of learning children accomplish in the first few years of their lives. They progress from Shakespeare's mewling and puking infant to his shining morning-faced schoolboy, and by and large, on the way, *they* have decided what counts, what interests them, what they want to master; by and large, they have owned their own learning. Their learning at this pre-school stage is relevant to them, purposeful, broad in its range and supported within a loving relationship. This means it is unhurried, and it occasions delight at all signs of development. Crucially, because they own it, their learning always begins from where they are.

"Learners come to school eager to learn and wanting to be taken seriously, to be esteemed for being who they are, with a need to be uplifted and challenged, with a desire to test their powers and stretch their muscles."
('Core Curriculum for Primary, Secondary and Adult Education in Norway', 1994)

23

When the child enters formal education, what happens to all this? Is it not the sad case that today, both teacher and child are trapped in a curriculum of prescribed content? To make matters worse, the curriculum is not just prescribed, but based on age-related assumptions, and shot through with pressure to achieve test results. One practical consequence of all this? A dramatic fall-off in the delight quotient!

In which case, what has the making of books got to offer schools? Can it be a means of retaining some of the factors which enable so much successful pre-school learning to take place?

In the name of Max, and all that is to be cherished, we believe it can!

We believe it can engender ownership, a sense of purpose, opportunities for choice, the requirement to make decisions, open-ended learning, motivation, discovery, first-hand experience, an exemplary working atmosphere, pleasure and fun in learning and delight at its product!

For the making of books is a process which for us is the living-out of certain beliefs. It is a process which pays fundamental respect to the integrity of the child as a learner. The child becomes central in the process, and is the prime mover, rather than a passive, possibly reluctant, recipient.

However, the teacher's role in the process is no soft option; rather, the teacher's knowledge, approach, sensitivities and understandings will be crucial. Clearly they will be crucial in, for example, choice of theme, the planning with colleagues and children, the preparation of classroom and resources, and the overseeing of the actual art and craft of the bookmaking.

With all this in mind, consider the reality. The teacher is the one who knows the children. The teacher is the mentor, the guide, the critical friend. The teacher, with or without help from other adults, encourages, demonstrates, advises, prompts and praises; instructs, asks relevant questions, sets standards, challenges assumptions, rejoices in success and identifies and meets needs. In the final reckoning it is the teacher who, in school, is responsible for each child's progress, success and self-esteem.

And there are some who would dare to regard this as a soft option!

> "Education must counteract fragmentary and compartmentalised learning...It confers tangs of one's talents, where everyone can find something they can master and so surprise even themselves...The most

important pre-condition here is a respect for the pupils' integrity, a sensitivity for their uniqueness and an urge to assist pupils in exploiting their potential and enticing them into their own borderland."
('Core Curriculum for Primary, Secondary and Adult Education in Norway', 1994)

But to return to Max, and to his classmates. He and they knew their journeys' destinations. They were each making a book. Pages would be selected from the range of colours available. Chosen pieces of work would be mounted. A contents page would be designed, and a title page and an 'about the author' page also. Each book would be sewn together, and then bound. Finally, covers would be added – covers which each child had printed or marbled or otherwise designed. An individual's efforts – a completed book – a journey's end?

We knew, of course, that two days might well be insufficient for all this thinking and reading and discussion – and deciding and doing and re-doing: and so it proved to be for several children. What of the adult, about whom we write in Chapter 10, *'The Teacher, The Learner'*? He ran out of time too, and returned later, as soon as he was able, to complete his journey. He was unaccompanied, but not alone, for the children were around and about.

All were given ample opportunity to work to the very highest level of their own skills, understanding and development. Importantly, there was no pressure to constrict any task into an arbitrary time scale. The work was finished when the artist, the writer, the researcher, the craftsman, the learner, deemed it to be finished. Thus it is – or should be – for any artist, writer, researcher, craftsman or learner.

The rock came out of a cave. I bought the rock in Dorset. My Auntie Lynn lives there so I went on holiday, and I bought it for my collection.

It has got rings like a tree trunk. My Blue John is opaque. It is purple with a little cream. It is mostly smooth but on the edge is rough. It is flat and very thin. It has different shades of purple.
(Emma)

Despite the limitations of time, a balance of sorts was achieved because of the planned range of activities. Creative skills were called on: drawing, painting, poetry, design. Scientific skills were called on, particularly that of detailed observation through microscopes and lenses. Mathematics (measuring, weighing, comparing), library and organisational skills, and of course handwriting, were all called on.

In fact, throughout a year's work, bookmaking can be a powerful means of addressing the magnificent aspirations of national legislation; of implementing a broad and balanced curriculum, which:

> "promotes the spiritual, moral, cultural, mental and physical development of pupils at school and of society...prepares pupils for the opportunities, responsibilities and experiences of adult life..."
> (Education Reform Act, 1988)

Clearly, our theme at Wimbotsham for those two days was primarily aesthetic, but it offered opportunities – which were taken – for wider exploration and reflection, confirming the truth that children do not think and learn in tightly controlled and defined 'subjects', but bring the totality of their experiences, themselves, to all of their thinking and learning.

BARK

> Bark is like a shield or thick skin. My grandad says that a green plant always grows on the north side of a tree, so it can help as a compass because the plant can't take the sun. Leaves bud in the spring because it starts to get warmer.
> (Max)

Bookmaking is a rich, helpful process. It involves regular discussion with peers and adults about particulars of the journey, and about detailed work in progress. Intrinsically, the children are involved in doing things which they have chosen to do because of the relevance of those things to their needs.

In the case of Max and the other Wimbotsham children, the journey involved growing knowledge and understanding of the chosen object. In all cases, it involves growing knowledge and understanding of some of what it means to be a learner – the need to confront concerns, to overcome emotional blockages, to cope both with successes and shortfalls, to be prepared to draft and re-draft, to persevere.

In the light of all of which, we can only wonder at and be saddened by the following huge misrepresentation as offered to readers of a national newspaper:

"...the influence of child-centred theories of education. Many teachers have been encouraged to believe children learn best when they find things out for themselves and that didactic teaching is inappropriate and inefficient. They believe their job is more to help children become 'independent learners' than to teach them the basic skills and subjects they need to know if they are to be educated people. The practical consequence of such beliefs is tedium and triviality."
(Chris Woodhead. The Observer, 22nd June 1997)

Oh dear: who is living in what world? During our two days with the children of Wimbotsham, the journey they made, and the manner in which they were allowed to make it, gave every child a sense of achievement, and a pride in the results; but it gave much more: of overriding importance, along with each child's fulfilment came *a commitment to the learning process itself* – and to the class, the teacher, and the school. Bookmaking is indeed a rich and powerfully enabling process.

"...the total pattern of findings indicates the strong probability that the associations between school process and outcome reflect in part a causal process. In other words, to an appreciable extent, children's behaviour and attitudes are shaped and influenced by their experiences at school and, in particular, by the qualities of the school as a social institution."
(Rutter, Maughan, Mortimore & Ousten: 'Fifteen Thousand Hours – Secondary Schools and Their Effects on Children')

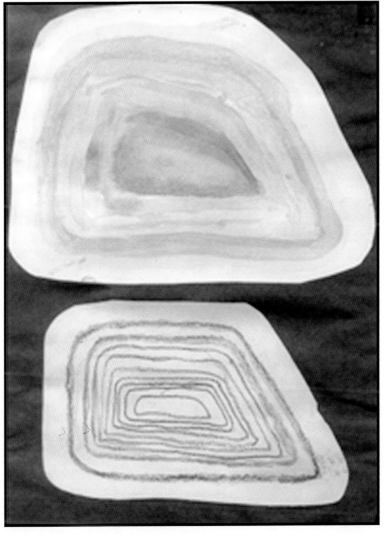

Blue John: **It has got rings like a tree trunk...**
It has shades of purple (Emma)

Chapter 8

THE MATTER OF TIME

"Like Piaget, Froebel felt that knowledge acquired by the young child had to be gradually sifted and that the child had to absorb concepts at his own rate of speed. Above all, Froebel believed in the innate capacity of a child to handle a certain amount of freedom. He thought that a teacher should follow in the wake of a child's intellectual development and not try to impose his own disciplines and tempo upon him arbitrarily."
(Ruth Inglis)

Two days (and more) studying a stone. Two days (and more) studying a feather. Two days (and more) studying a bit of bark. Two days (and more)...

At a recent meeting for school governors, we heard it claimed on behalf of the literacy hour that because it was structured in distinct parts, and because each part had a distinctive content, the children would not therefore become bored with any one activity, nor with the hour.

But at Wimbotsham we saw learning and application and commitment and concentration and interest and enthusiasm and enjoyment sustained throughout two days...and beyond. Lady Rose Hare, the chairman of the school's governors, who was able to be with us just for the afternoon of Day Two, wrote to us afterwards of *"the sense of commitment, fun, concentration and pure enjoyment (which) came across to me so strongly."*

"...boys and girls of 7, 8 and 9 do remain long absorbed in the activity of the moment; and if an activity fails to absorb their attention on its own account, any claim for its value as a preparation for the future usually leaves them unmoved."
(Christian Schiller)

29

Two days (and more) studying a wasps' nest. Two days (and more) studying a bit of rock. Two days (and more) studying a shell. Two days (and more)...

A couple of weeks later, when the children were asked about the two days, 6 said that two days was about the right length of time, 21 said that it was not long enough, and just a single child said that she found it too long. (Significantly, this child had been absent on Day One, and so had missed the whole of the vital first leg of the journey.)

It was at once salutary and disturbing to watch Richard on mid-afternoon of Day Two, still working prodigiously on his wasps' nest, to know that from the forthcoming September at his secondary school he will find his pattern of learning determined less by himself and his needs and preferences, more by the ringing of a school bell, and organisational convenience. *"Books away now,"* says the teacher of Geography; *"off you go to Maths. See you next week."*

The secondary school timetable is indeed a process of continuous abortion, but it was equally disturbing to realise that had Richard not been attending his particular primary school, but any one of many others, he probably would not have had to wait until secondary school before his needs became so subordinated to those of the institution. Clearly there are no easy answers; any school will be bound to suffer from the limitations of organisational requirements. Nevertheless, the needs of the learner and the nature of learning must be allowed to remain paramount, so that it is the normal course of events for them to take precedence over organisational requirements.

It is a humbling thought that every single day of our lives we are the inheritors, the beneficiaries, the ignorant users, of many thousands of years of human achievement, of human intelligence applied. What we eat, what we wear, what we drink, how we travel, how we communicate, what we take or are given to get well, how we cook, how we address our personal hygiene...every day of our lives. A litany of names could be recited; a roll call of the illustrious could march across this and many another page...for our forebears grafted, gritted teeth, pondered, persevered in the face of incredulity and persecution, enjoyed flashes of inspiration along with agonies of perspiration...all in the cause of progress.

Invariably, to do this they had to understand, really understand, their subject; not superficially, but profoundly. To do this, they needed time: time to think, time to go inside and outside and all around their subject, time to discuss with others, time to try things out – to make mistakes and learn from them.

At what stage in a child's formal education is this attribute of time made available? Is it ever made available, in the terms we have just described? Is it at all *possible*, at primary level, at secondary level? Our two-day journey with the children of Wimbotsham leads us to believe that not to give the child at least a taste of real learning time is to deny the child a vital educational experience. If it is all a White Rabbit rush: rush to get the rudiments in, rush to get the facts in, rush to get that-which-will-be-tested in, rush from one subject to another, from one teacher to another, time-piece ever to hand, how is the child supposed ever to dwell on anything, to think through anything, to internalise anything...to reach out towards his/her potential?

At *what* stage in a child's formal education is the attribute of time made available?

Junior education minister Mrs. Margaret Hodge announced on 19th February 1999 that *"We are modernising the early years. We need to bring together play, care, and education in a structured and rigorous way which is appropriate to the age of the child."* Notwithstanding these ominous sentiments, it should be cause for thought that pre-school learning is not usually accomplished within a context of rigid and limited time allocations. Nor indeed is the learning we derive from our adult days. Instead, both of these are largely determined by the needs of the learner and according to a greater flexibility than is generally the norm in schools. Strange then that learning between the ages of 4/5 and 18 should be regarded so differently.

The irony extends to the testing in schools of children's learning. How, other than to wonder where ultimately all of this might lead, are we to respond to a report from the Qualifications and Curriculum Authority in which, with apparent seriousness, it regrets that many seven and eleven year olds are hindered by *"poor test technique"* which causes them to *"manage their time badly and leave questions unfinished"*! (Times Educational Supplement report, 18th December 1998)

> *"Only a few years ago we used to come to England, to see how you do things. What happened?"*
> *(A German teacher, quoted in the N.A.H.T. Head Teachers' Review, Spring 1994)*

Two days (and more) studying a teasel. Two days (and more) studying a horse's tooth. Two days (and more) studying a fossil. Two days (and more)...

"Recent proposals to divide the school year into shorter but more numerous terms ignore the fact that from the point of view of the consumer of education – the child – any such change will leave the education system as flawed as it was before.

Real children don't learn efficiently in the way which the compulsory school system assumes they do. Childhood is not a time in people's lives when they learn easily in rigid blocks of instruction. They don't become enthusiastic about, say, French between two arbitrarily chosen moments, only to close their minds to it completely when the bell calls them to plunge into Maths or Geography..."
(Christopher R. Shute. The Observer, 31st January 1999)

One almost might

Wouldn't you say,
Wouldn't you say: one day,
With a little more time or a little more patience, one might
Disentangle for separate, deliberate, slow delight
One of the moment's hundred strands, unfray
Beginnings from endings, this from that, survey
Say a square inch of the ground one stands on, touch
Part of oneself or a leaf or a sound (not clutch
Or cuff or bruise but touch with finger-tip, ear-
Tip, eyetip, creeping near yet not too near);
Might take up life and lay it on one's palm
And, encircling it in closeness, warmth and calm,
Let it lie still, then stir smooth-softly, and
Tendril by tendril unfold, there on one's hand...

One might examine eternity's cross-section
For a second, with slightly more patience, more time for reflection?
(A. S. J. Tessimond)

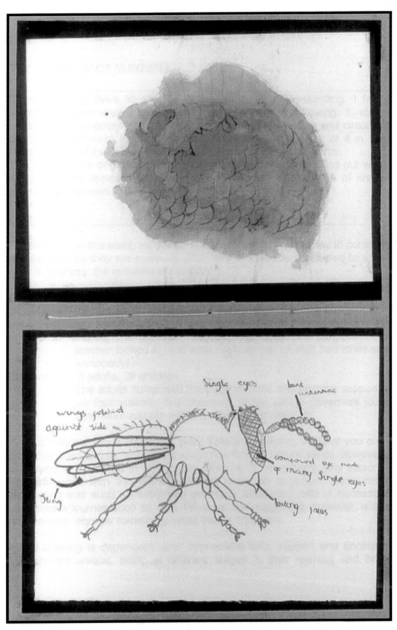

Wasps' Nest: It was at once salutary and disturbing to watch Richard on mid-afternoon of Day Two still working prodigiously on his wasps' nest...

Chapter 9

THE QUESTION OF NUMBERS

"It may help to have in mind what we mean by understanding. I feel I understand something if and when I can do some, at least, of the following: 1. state it in my own words; 2. give examples of it; 3. recognise it in various guises and circumstances; 4. see connections between it and other facts or ideas; 5. make use of it in various ways; 6. foresee some of its consequences; 7. state its opposite or converse.

This list is only a beginning; but it may help us in the future to find out what our students really know as opposed to what they can give the appearance of knowing; their real learning as opposed to their apparent learning."
(John Holt)

Forgive us if, at this point, we pause in our account of our journey to consider these words of John Holt, for they are profound. Also, they are directly connected to an issue which we want to address: the question of numbers.

Day One:

7 adults. 27 children.
The adults comprised the class teacher, the learning support assistant, we four visitors, and a visiting teacher present for just this one day. For part of the day also the local methodist minister and the peripatetic learning support teacher looked in, and soon realised that all they had to do was sit down by somebody!

Day Two:

6 adults. 28 children.
The adults comprised the class teacher, the learning support assistant, and we four visitors. The chairman of the school governors joined us for the afternoon, and sat with a number of the children.

Yes – a *very* generous adult/pupil ratio! Totally unrealistic, we hear you cry! Well, we will meet that point shortly, and others which flow from it; before we do, however, and before it is allowed to invalidate in substantial measure, if not entirely, any lessons to be drawn from our work with the children, let us make an important disclaimer. We are not suggesting that such an extremely generous adult/pupil ratio is necessary, in order to undertake a journey such as ours. What we are suggesting, however, is that John Holt's *real learning* requires something better than a 1/30 ratio.

If real learning is dependent upon appropriate help, support and encouragement; if all learners are unique, being at different stages in their learning and bringing different strengths and weaknesses to their learning, then clearly the notion of one class, one teacher/adult makes huge demands.

So where is the poor, beleaguered class teacher to turn to for help? A cause for optimism has been the recognition by the government in its Green Paper *'Teachers: Meeting The Challenge of Change'* (December 1998) that: *"Teaching assistants are playing an increasingly important role in schools."* The government proposes that an additional 20,000 full-time (or equivalent) assistants will be provided for schools by the year 2002. Indeed, the DfEE has already honoured the Green Paper commitment to produce *"guidance in the use of teaching assistants based on existing good and innovative practice."*

Meanwhile, parents, friends, governors, retired colleagues, students, the local clergy...all could be approached. Just a couple of helpers could well push the team up from the one teacher to four adults, with the aid of the school's own learning support assistant.

Other questions crowd in, here:

Who would 'train' these helpers?
How would they be 'trained'?
What part, if any, would they play in planning?
What if they were not available on a regular basis?

What if they proved unsuitable?

The question of 'training' is very important, and it contains within it a subsidiary question – what would be required of these volunteers, who would not be qualified teachers? They would certainly want to know that themselves, before agreeing to help, and in the answer would lie the seeds of the training. However, let us be clear about one thing in this connection: the Wimbotsham team of six adults was cohesive, and the strong bond that united the team resided in their belief in children, and in the nature of the learning process, but *all were individuals*. To draw on Fullan and Hargreaves: *"The teacher as a person:"* the times in which they grew up, and entered the profession, the dominant values and educational beliefs that went with those times; how teaching was bound up with the rest of their lives and interests; the actual stage their skills and experience had reached – *different*, in each case.

In the case of the learning support assistant of course, very different. She was a young mother of young children. She was not a qualified teacher, but she *was* a superb member of the team in the way she related to the children.

So the question of being trained up to the job is not a finite one. Training in the skills of teaching is infinitely on-going. Perhaps 'preparation' is a more useful concept, when considering the use of volunteer adults in the classroom, and however that preparation is implemented, it really does need to focus on the key issues of attitudes to children, and to the nature of the learning process: on how children learn, and how they should be treated.

An initial discussion with the adult (ideally *after* he/she has had the opportunity to sit in on a classroom session); letting the volunteer sit in on a planning session; helping and guiding him/her 'on the job'; ensuring de-briefing and review sessions: it might all sound a huge task, but in reality it need not be, because by its very nature it will be spread over time. The potential rewards certainly justify the time and effort.

> *At one point I was a dull and rough amethyst, then one day I was dug up. I was put in a large round cylinder and I didn't know what it was. I got pushed in with some grit, then soaked by some water. I was in here for a week. Then the tumbling was still repeated, only smaller finer grits. Then eventually I was finished. All rounded, polished and smoothen. Then put out for jewellery.*
> *(Kaylee)*

35

If adult helpers are not regularly available, that should not rule them out altogether; do not let the best be the enemy of the good, as someone once wrote! Give them due notice, and use them when they can make it. As they gain experience as part of a team, their support will be valuable even if it has to be occasional...if they are up to it. If they are not? The answer to this lies in the nature of their unsuitability, and clearly some difficult situations could arise, requiring both tact and firmness, but one has to ask if concern at this possibility should be allowed to stop all attempts to obtain extra adult help.

We would note that, to our knowledge, very many schools are positive in their attempts to attract adults into the classroom, and many children benefit as a result. For, to an important extent, it *is* a question of numbers. We find it a matter of concern and astonishment that there are those (and not only those who hold the purse strings!) who regard class size, and adult/pupil ratios, as relatively insignificant. For John Holt's real learning to take place, children need adults to talk with; they need an adult alongside them, to help them: to put things into their own words, to search for examples, to recognise things in various guises, to see connections, uses, consequences...yes, in a vital sense, it *is* a question of numbers!

> *"Teacher: two kinds: the kind that fill you with so much quail shot that you can't move, and the kind that just give you a little prod behind and you jump to the skies."*
> (Robert Frost)

Chapter 10

THE TEACHER, THE LEARNER

"I'm not a teacher: only a fellow-traveller of whom you asked the way. I pointed ahead – ahead of myself as well as of you."
(George Bernard Shaw)

Our planning sessions in the time running up to the two days with the children were revealing. As we shared our ideas about children and our ideas about learning, we found that the secondary-orientated individual amongst us tended to be product-focused. The primary-orientated, however, were process-focused. The secondary-orientated tended to think in terms of finite skills which either were or were not possessed by people. The primary-orientated thought in terms of potential. A snatch of dialogue, and its outcome, will illustrate the point.

"But what of the children who can't sketch or paint? Won't our requirement that they do so, inevitably turn some of them off? Blunt their enthusiasm? Make them feel inadequate at the very outset?"

"Everybody can sketch. Everybody can paint."

"I can't."

"Yes you can."

"Believe me, I'm telling you, I CANNOT!"

"Believe me, I'm telling you, YOU CAN!"

So, not convinced, he very reluctantly agreed to sit with the children, and do what they were asked to do. He sketched his Chinese lantern. He mixed a luscious orangey-red paint and he painted a portrait of his Chinese lantern.

All the time, memories from fifty years ago came back to haunt him. The Art lesson. The Geography teacher in charge. The cane – for using a ruler! The feeling of utter, embarrassing ineptitude.

But now, the children at his table, and from various corners of the room, came over (for they had been told of his profound sense of inadequacy), put a hand on his shoulder, and said complimentary things about his sketch, and about his painting. The primary colleague who had *told* him at that planning meeting that he could sketch, that he could paint, stood at his side for a moment and with a quiet word indicated how his sketch could be completed.

He felt, but concealed, a sense of achievement. The level of concentration exhausted him, yet playtime was an unlooked-for interruption. He would soon learn that whilst the pleasure in the product was delicious but ephemeral, the experience of the process, and what it did for him, was much, much longer-lasting.

You need not see what someone is doing
to know if it is his vocation.
You only have to watch his eyes:
a cook mixing a sauce, a surgeon
making a primary incision,
a clerk completing a bill of lading,
wear the same rapt expression,
forgetting themselves in a function...
There should be monuments, there should be odes...
To the first flaker of flints who forgot his dinner,
To the first collector of sea shells to remain celibate...
(W. H. Auden)

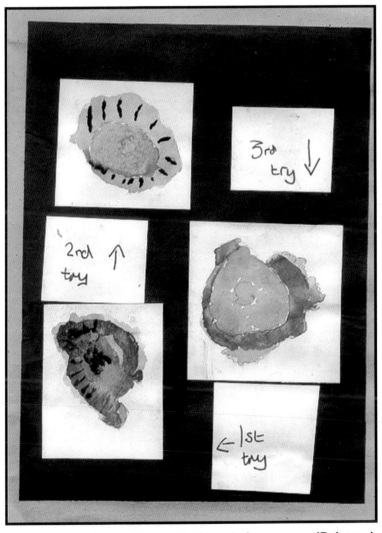

Fossil: 1st try, 2nd try, 3rd try   (Rebecca)

Chapter 11

THE STONE

"Below my window in Ross where I'm working the blossom is out in full...it's the whitest, frothiest, blossomest blossom that there ever could be. And things are more trivial than they ever were and more important than they ever were and the difference doesn't seem to matter. The nowness of everything is absolutely wondrous...The fact is that if you see the present tense, boy do you see it! And boy can you celebrate it."
(Dennis Potter, in his final television interview, 1994)

'Just a bit of bark?'
(Max: his book title)

The stone he had brought in was diabolical. It was the dullest, the most pathetic, the most uninteresting stone I honestly believe I have ever seen in my life. It had absolutely nothing to commend it: not size, not shape, not colour, not composition. Nothing.

Two days with that thing? God forfend the moment, let alone the days, I thought! A roughly-oval sketch, a dropped blob of dirty brown paint, a quick flip through an illustrated library book and a line of...prose? poetry? despair?! And that's it. The art, the research and the creative writing all done – before morning playtime most likely.

I do believe he had *forgotten* to select a natural object to bring with him to school that day. In haste, in panic, in a supreme act of indifference, who knows, he probably picked up the first thing that came to hand as he meandered his dreamy way in. The result – that stone!

All around him were gorgeous peacock feathers, huge fossils, tiny gemstones, gnarled chunks of wood, winking rocks shot through with quartz, and dozens more inspiring objects...and there he sat, with his stone. My own heart turned to stone, but I put on a brave face and approached him.

"Ah, Scott, your stone. Now you are ready to write about it."

Silence. We both gazed at the thing before us.

"Where did it come from?"

"The beach."

(A likely story!) *"Oh, the beach. What was it resting on, on the beach?"*

"Sand."

"What was the sand like?"

"Soft."

A man of few words, our Scott. My questions were well spaced out, and tip-toed forward as if over egg shells. I had no idea where Scott was coming from. He certainly felt no need to fill our silences.

"Soft. Soft as what?"

"Soft as a cushion."

"So, the stone was lying on a soft cushion of sand. Right. What was the sea doing? Was the tide in? Was it rough or calm?"

"Rough."

"Rough. Right! So the waves were..."

"Crashing!"

(Is that a light I see coming into your eyes, young man?) *"Crashing. The waves were crashing."*

"And splashing."

"And splashing! Now Scott, I begin to see why you brought this object in. You found it lying on a soft cushion of sand, alongside crashing, splashing waves. That was where it belonged?"

"Yes. It belonged there. Now it's stolen..."

Scott, Scott, that *is* a light in your eyes. You are alive and into it now, aren't you! Forget Lizzie's peacock feather alongside you. Forget Edward's complete wing of a mallard opposite you. You've got your stone, and it's got its story. Come on Scott, let's go...

And go we did. What a story. It had atmosphere. It had plot. It had emotion. Words, ideas, were conjured forth, and a story was born of the unlikeliest stone in the world.

A stone, sitting on the soft cushion of sand by the screaming, squawking, screeching seagulls. Through the hot summers and the cold winter frosts.

STOLEN!

Now it is in a cruel person's garden. No seagulls. No waves. What can I do?

You are doing it, Scott, writer, of Wimbotsham: you are doing it!

"Down through the ages and in the whole world, Watt and Newton cannot have been the only ones to notice the steam from a boiling kettle or observe an apple fall.

Having eyes, but not seeing beauty: having ears, but not hearing music: having minds, but not perceiving truth: having hearts that are never moved and therefore never set on fire. These are the things to fear, said the Headteacher."
(From Totto-chan, by Tetsuko Kuroyanagi.)

41

Just a bit of bark?   **(Max)**

Chapter 12

THE DISAGREEMENT

> *"We should not pretend that everyone can be a writer, nor build illusions that lead only to frustration. For only a few will be true writers. Some will be successful, others fail. But those few will find fulfilment in the richest form of creativity I know."*
> *('Authors are born, not made': an article by Professor Malcolm Bradbury in The Observer, 29th November 1998)*

We agree, Professor Bradbury. Authors are born. Every day.

We fear, however, that we are agreeing at cross purposes. We say this, because it seems to us that you know exactly what you mean by *"authors"*; you mean Chaucer, Shakespeare, Milton, Defoe, Swift, Fielding, Dickens... For you, these are the men to be numbered amongst the *"few...true writers"*. For you, *"those few will find fulfilment in the richest form of creativity I know."*

We are tempted to suggest that you offer that encomium to literature to Beethoven, or Rembrandt or Michelangelo, or any number of artists supreme in spheres other than literature, but that is not our argument at the moment...instead, we suggest that you tell that to the children of Wimbotsham County Primary School.

They write, you see. In fact, they don't, to use your words: *"pretend that everyone can be a writer;"* they *know* it! They would react with astonishment to your eristical suggestion that writing is some form of esoteric skill given to a select few. They simply would not understand what you were saying. They write, you see, all of them. They give thought to their subject, they explore the words and ideas which might be useful and relevant to a treatment of their subject, they research their subject; just as they did during our two days with them.

They each brought in a natural object, studied it, and wrote about it. They *worked* on their writing of course; draft after draft; nobody produced the finished piece first time. Each produced his/her finished piece eventually, however. They realised that the time frame for creating a piece of writing is not to be found on the face of a clock, and so those who had not achieved what they had hoped to achieve on the first day were not discouraged.

Indeed, it has been known for some of them to re-visit a topic days or weeks later, when they know they have something they want to write.

By and large, however, in the case of those two days, the work of creating a piece of writing was achieved by all. Each vividly illustrates the eye and the mind of the child. Some show the child grappling with the structure of a story. Some show the child delighting in a word, or words.

Some seem pedestrian, to put it mildly, but pedestrian to us, as adults; for all that, they represent for children the first, small steps into the art and craft of writing. Surely the vital point is, that the children *are* undertaking the task. Nobody has told them that they are *not* writers, that they *cannot* be writers, that they *never ever will be* writers because not everyone can be!

Forget illusions. Forget dreams of best-sellers and fantasies of fortunes. We are not talking about the lottery of getting published, let alone the bigger lottery of being published with the right marketing, at the right time, in the right place. No. We are talking about the encouragement of children to observe, to reflect, to commit words to paper; to explore, in words; to come to terms with feelings and events and sadnesses and joy...in words; to recognise the power of words to make us laugh or cry, or see or sigh. Like Emily.

> *MY SHELL*
>
> *My shell came from Devon. When I was on holiday I found it in 1997 in the summer.*
>
> *It is special to me because I have had it for a very long while and it used to have pretty colours on it but now it has got worn out. But you can still see some pretty colours.*
>
> *The shell is very big and I also have a small shell just like this shell but it has more colours on it.*
>
> *My shell is a mussel shell.*

THE OLD LADY BEACH SHELL

Inside my old lady beach shell
Are all pretty colours
It's like an old lady
She was pretty when she was young
But
When she is old
She gets less pretty
But
Some of her pretty bits are left
And that is my old lady beach shell.
(Emily)

We want our children to see themselves as writers throughout their lives. We want to give them that belief, and that birthright. To this end we will support and encourage and outrageously applaud them. We will strive to give them such self-belief that when their head, or their heart, or both, need or want to express what is carried therein, then they will not hesitate to pick up the pen and find the paper.

Seamus Heaney has talked of writing aiding the *alignment of self*, where so much else in life scatters. It is in the exploring and the expressing that our children will find themselves – and others – and much more besides. A stone is just a stone until it becomes a story: we know that don't we, Scott – writer of Wimbotsham!

"In the Meno, one of Plato's great dialogues, have you read it Lieu-
tenant, Socrates demonstrates that a slave boy can learn the
principles of geometry as well as a gentleman...

In other words, he shows that human beings have an intelligence
which has nothing to do with the circumstances into which they are
born...

Sit down Lieutenant. It is a matter of reminding the slave of what he
knows, of his own intelligence. And by intelligence you may read
goodness, talent, the innate qualities of human beings...

When he treats the slave boy as a rational human being, the boy
becomes one, he loses his fear, and he becomes a competent
mathematician. A little more encouragement and he might become an
extraordinary mathematician. Who knows?"
(Timberlake Wertenbaker, 'Our Country's Good')

45

Chapter 13

THE LOGISTICAL PROBLEMS

"Good teaching gets learning started – but it is consummated by the learner's own efforts...Good teaching will give pupils evidence of succeeding in their work, faith in their own abilities, and the heart to take responsibility for their own learning and their own lives."
('Core Curriculum for Primary, Secondary and Adult Education in Norway', 1994)

Day 1:

We had completed our whole-class introductory talk/discussion. Most children would be beginning with art work – drawing or painting – and would need to collect their chosen paper and the other materials required. The paper, of various colours and already cut to appropriate sizes, was arranged in a number of storage trays along one side of the classroom. This was likely to be the only time on this day when there would be considerable simultaneous movement around the classroom by very many children and when that movement would be concentrated in and towards one particular part of the classroom.

How could this best be accomplished with the minimum of disruption and disturbance to those who had begun working and for whom an accidental knock could spoil their work?

The problem was described to the children.

A solution suggested by Michael: that the children should go one table at a time to collect their paper and other materials; that those who had to wait should be prepared to do so knowing that any impatience that they felt would be in a good cause.

Supplement to solution suggested by one of the adults present: that children sitting at the side of the classroom furthest from the art papers should be the first to collect, and that those sitting the nearest should be the last; thus should further be minimised the possibility of work being spoiled because of a child being jolted.

Solution agreed. Logistical problem solved.

Day 2:

The completed art work and writing, with the owner's name written (we hoped!) on the back of each sheet, had until now been placed for safe keeping in a single storage tray which contained at least one piece of work by each of the 28 children. All of this work now had to be returned to its various owners so that it could be mounted in readiness for fixing into their books. Without some sort of system this had the potential for relative mayhem and for damage to the pieces of work.

The problem was described to the children.

A number of solutions were suggested, none of which met with unanimous or even significant majority approval. So, as time allowed us to do so, it was agreed to postpone a final decision.

It was on revisiting the problem that Scott suggested that a few children should return the completed work to its various owners while the other children remained seated. After further discussion it was agreed that all children should also be given paper clips with which to keep their pages together, and that all children should from that point on assume responsibility for their own papers. They would keep them until needed, either in their own storage tray or in the communal tray in which they were presently kept or in some other safe place of their own choosing.

Solution agreed. Logistical problem solved.

Let us reflect upon the importance of what has been described, for it may, on first reading, appear trivial.

In fact in both cases, the solution to a problem which concerned every child had been offered by a child and had been accepted by the remainder of the children. There was amongst the children a sense of ownership of the problem and of the solution.

The solution was not a teacher's solution. Perhaps as far as children are concerned teachers are too often offering solutions, and they see this as part of the teacher's role. Teachers' solutions are too often not a matter for negotiation!

But in the cases we have described the solutions were children's solutions. They had become corporate solutions. They were sensible and workable. They were not solutions imposed by the teacher, who is expected to offer solutions. Perhaps it was for these reasons that our two significant logistical problems were successfully resolved.

Therefore, far from being trivial, these two cases go to the heart of the matter; they are part of the bedrock upon which our journey prospered.

> "The young must gradually shoulder more responsibility for the planning and achievement of their own education – and they must take responsibility for their own conduct and behaviour."
> ('Core Curriculum for Primary, Secondary and Adult Education in Norway', 1994)

Woodlice   **(Lee)**

Chapter 14

THE TITLE PAGE (A Cautionary Tale)

"Even while they teach, men learn."
(Seneca)

The children were each making a book. Surely we were all familiar enough with books not to need to linger long over their conventions and their characteristics – except perhaps for a few words with the whole class concerning the 'about the author' page and the title page.

A discussion took place, therefore, about what details concerning the author might be of interest to the reader; about a suggestion from Richard that they might also include a photograph of the author; and then about the particular and unaccustomed challenge of writing about oneself in the third person.

And so we came to the title page – a necessary cause for pause because, as far as the adult who was leading this particular discussion was concerned, he doubted it to be something with which even the more voracious of our young readers were likely to be overly familiar.

The classroom was, of course, substantially stocked with books, but crucially no title page from even one of those books was examined. We remain uncertain about the reason for this omission, though we think that it owed more to omission by accident rather than to a deliberate decision.

Either way, we did not use a single one of all the books that were around us. Instead, by question and answer, we identified together those things which might customarily be found on the title page of a book; and, as we did so, we constructed the following simple guide on the classroom whiteboard:

Title

Author

Illustrator

First Published

Address

All of it was entirely honourable, in the good intentions of which it basks here on the printed page as proudly as it did on the classroom whiteboard!

However, it should not have come as a surprise, though it was a disappointment, to discover a little later that a number of title pages had been completed in a similar way to that in which Rebecca had completed hers:

Title:	Me and my fossil
Author:	Rebecca Walker
Illustrator:	Rebecca Walker
First published:	1998
Address:	Downham Road, Runcton Holme, King's Lynn, Norfolk.

This appeared instead of the conventional presentation which had been our intention when discussing it, a presentation which could have been found in any one of the classroom's many books.

We had caused the children to neglect the first-hand experience/evidence which was immediately available in their trays and on their classroom bookshelves; we had ignored the potential gap between the intended meanings of speaker and the received meanings of listener. Some children had made an error of presentation. It could and probably would have been avoided if they had been allowed to discover for themselves, with assistance if appropriate, the scarcely complicated conventions of title pages. The independent learner, he/she whose learning is properly rooted in first hand experience, would surely have succeeded where the over-directed had failed.

So, well-intentioned teacher, being teacher, got it wrong, failing the children in this specific instance.

"To teach is to learn."
(Japanese Proverb)

Chapter 15

THE EXPERIENCE

"To me education is a leading out of what is already there in the pupil's soul."
(Muriel Spark)

Not once. Not twice. Many times. And every time, with all primary age groups, it works. The children become story tellers and writers.

In a way, the fact that we are talking about one aspect of the curriculum is irrelevant; the fact that we are talking about one aspect of the curriculum is incidental to the educational principles at stake. For what we are doing is – believing in children; drawing out from children; the process *is* e-ducare; a leading out; education.

The well is not dry. Children see, hear, feel, touch, smell, with an avidity lost to most adults. They look around with a curiosity that has been dulled in most adults. They explore to the point of danger, and all their experiences flow into them through an open sluicegate. There is constant enrichment and discovery, and there is constant growth. It is a mistake to imagine that they do their 'learning' solely, or chiefly, at school.

They do their national curriculum at school. *How* that is done, the *relationships* the doing is based on, the *attitudes* colouring the efforts to achieve certain 'levels', the whole approach to the concepts of 'success' and 'failure'; these are the things which will be remembered, these are the things which will go deep. For good or ill, these are the powerful, formative influences on the developing child.

"This suggests that the way children are taught can make a difference to their general development as well as to the production of academic ability...

...that schooling ought not to be assessed solely on the basis of reading and maths ability. There might be economic returns to thinking more imaginatively about the role of schooling and the way schools interact with families and children in generating well-educated, productive, but also well-rounded and confident individuals...

...that schooling should not be too narrowly assessed...

There is also, clearly, two-way causality between educational ability and psychological attributes such as self-esteem, the development of each facilitating the development of the other..."
(Analysis of the data from the 1970 British Cohort Study, a major longitudinal study of all the children born in the U.K. in the first week of April 1970, and surveyed again in 1975, 1980, 1986, 1991 and 1996. Published by the London School of Economics and Political Science, 1999)

The teacher who is prepared to be a learner too, in the eyes of the children; the teacher who *expects* the children to be writers, mathematicians, scientists, sportsfolk; the teacher who retains the enthusiasm and open-heartedness of a lost youth: that teacher, that believer in children, will not be disappointed.

"Education is not the filling of a pail, but the lighting of a fire."
(W. B. Yeats)

"Every second we live is a new and unique moment of the universe, a moment that never was before and never will be again. And what do we teach children in school? We teach them that two and two make four and that Paris is the capital of France. We should say to each of them, 'Do you know what you are? You are a marvel. You are unique. In the millions of years that have passed, there has never been another child like you.'"
(Pablo Casals)

We are back at Wimbotsham now, in the classroom. Language work is under way. Words are suggested, drawn out. Ideas are thrown around. Carefully, to those who need it (as opposed to those who are inclined to want it without really needing it!), help is given. Questions are asked, quizzical eyebrows are raised, smiles radiate and *"Yesses"* reverberate, all in the context of the *child's* own efforts.

What efforts! The imaginative range, the comparisons fresh as new-laid eggs, the twists and turns of plot, the sheer delight in sounds and syllables! That which is produced is shown, shared, celebrated. We are in the world of realising potential, drawing it out so naturally that the children do not give a second's hesitation to discovering, studying, creating. They are writers.

> TEASEL
>
> *Prickly like a hedgehog*
> *Brown like a tree trunk*
> *Crispy like my cornflakes*
> *Pointed like a tree top*
> *Light like a feather*
> *Fragile like pottery*
> *Spiked like my grandad's beard.*
> *(Samantha B)*

Yes. They are writers. Later in the week they are going to be mathematicians, and then scientists, geographers, gymnasts, musicians...

> *"For children and adolescents, the world is new and nothing in it is taken for granted. They often grope and question matters that adults accept as a matter of course, and they have a rich ability to fantasise and an unfettered imagination. Reality sets few limits to their musings. Children's boundless inquisitiveness is a model for all who wish to develop and learn. It is also a quality of childhood that the school must cherish and make use of in teaching – since children learn to a large degree from each other...*
>
> *The learning environment must be both humane and loyal towards children's inquisitiveness. Learning to read and write, to do math (sic) and draw, experiment, play and analyse, should release a creative craving, not restrain it."*
> *('Core Curriculum for Primary, Secondary and Adult Education in Norway', 1994)*

Yes! Yes! Yes!

54

Quartz   **(Danny)**

Chapter 16

THE PLENARY

GEODE

Geode is a mineral and is found in Brazil.
My piece of geode could be thousands of years old.
True minerals are inorganic. All gemstones are minerals.
Gemstones are found under the sea or ground.
In pure form, a mineral is homogeneous — that is, every part of it is
the same as any other part.
(Samantha I)

Learning can be a lonely thing.

I have my desk; or I have my chair at the table and my tray of books and pens and pencils. I have room to lean my elbows amongst the forest of elbows all around. But where do I lean my mind? Or the elbows of my heart? They are locked inside. Nobody can touch them. Nobody can see them. They might peep out through a high, arrow-slit window now and then, but it would take a patient, keen observer ever to notice.

Almost all the tasks I do, I do alone. *My* pen. *My* paper. *My* work. By me, for me; resulting from what I have heard, from what I have seen, from what I have felt, from what I have understood.

Because my steed does not have unlimited stamina, I know I won't have galloped far into the golden realms of understanding or achievement. I might have reached their edge sometimes. But whatever destination I achieve, the journey is my own. No-one else can make it for me. Some wintry days I seem to be riding over very high mountains, and I make very little progress.

Some days the sun shines, the way forward is along the flowered banks of a great river of understanding, and my heart sings at the progress being made. Either way, I am on my own.

That is why I love the gathering.

Out of our desks. Out of our classrooms. Away from our tabled positions. Into the big, airy space of the hall, where all things seem possible. Other classes file in. Big circle. Expectant hush. Even Teacher's voice sounds different here, as we sit in an unbroken, curling line of expectancy. Look, the curtains are being drawn. We are all held in a pool of light in the midst of darkness.

Then it happens. We are all invited to share. The shell of isolation is cracked, and if we want to, and feel comfortable to, which almost all of us do because we are used to being handled sensitively, we share.

Poems, stories: long, short, illustrated, serious, humorous, halting, fluent, declaimed, whispered. Like Magi from the East, each of us brings our offering from its long journey, to be placed at the feet of the many. We all listen, for we never know what is coming next. Sometimes, out of the near darkness, a disembodied voice floats amongst us. Sometimes, one of the grown-ups reads what he has written. Whoever, whatever, we all applaud, none more than our Teachers whose faces shine with delight!

This is an *occasion*. Our work has merited an *occasion!*

> *DEAD OR ALIVE?*
>
> *The book says inorganic,*
> *that it isn't alive.*
> *But it dazzles,*
> *sparkles,*
> *and best of all it*
> *WINKS!*
> *So is my*
> *Brazilian beauty*
> *Dead – or alive?*
> *(Samantha I)*

Chapter 17

THE JOURNEY'S END...?

> *"Whether 30 years later anything happens will be because a teacher made a difference. The encounter takes on an almost spiritual dimension. The ripple of influence never stops."*
> *(Ernest Boyer)*

The journey's end might have been at the end of Day Two.

Or the journey's end might have been reached on various of the following few days as writing and artwork were finished and mounted and books were completed.

But perhaps the journey's end is never reached.

Perhaps the quality of the experience is such that it continues to reverberate down the days. Perhaps the quality of the response to the experience helps to make sense of, to define, to make permanent and to celebrate that experience; so that to try to identify endings is futile and is to miss the essence.

We do know, for example, that for Rebecca the ripples were continuing; that her journey had not ended a couple of days after some might have thought that it would have done:

"Mrs Foot, shall I...I don't think that I need to ask you that."

An exquisite moment! Rebecca blossoms.

Is it not a reasonable expectation that Max – he of *'Just a bit of bark?'* – will continue to recognise and to celebrate the extraordinariness of the ordinary?

And it is surely a reasonable expectation that other ripples of influence will also never stop; that there will be no journey's end:

> *"A teacher affects eternity; he can never tell where his influence stops."*
> *(Henry Brooks Adams)*

So why have we felt compelled to offer a portrait of our experience? (We certainly did not begin the journey with an intention to do so.) What claims are we making for what happened?

The nature of the portrait itself is the answer to those questions. Certainly, what we have written of those two days is not presented as a template, as a model for classroom and school practice which we would want others unthinkingly to adopt.

Instead, we hope that it might contribute to the continuing debate about education, especially – but not exclusively – the debate about primary education; that it might do so in a way that demonstrably links beliefs and values with practice; that in doing so we might give the debate a tug *in the direction of children*.

We wrote at the outset of a journey of faith; it is a faith in children. That faith takes courage to hold and time to come to fruition.

Sadly, it is in real and present danger of being crushed. The heavy, measuring, inflexible hand of so many current educational imperatives threatens. But our faith in children must be kept alive.

All our children must be allowed to grow, secure in a context of love and trust where all abilities and aptitudes are valued and celebrated and encouraged to flourish. The very best part of themselves must be fed, watered and nurtured every day, so that they can move confidently towards an adulthood, a wisdom, rooted in humanity.

Such faith will be rewarded, as surely as it was when we journeyed together with the children of Wimbotsham for those two glorious days.

> *FEATHER*
>
> *A feather as light ds air*
> *A feather as strong as metal*
> *A feather as soft as wool*
> *A feather as buoyant as cumulus in flight*
> *A feather as wonderful as magic*
> *Magical feather give me flight.*
> *(Edward)*

Magical feather give me flight   (Edward)

APPENDIX A

THE CHILDREN AND THEIR NATURAL OBJECTS

Adam	Flint
Clare	Fossil
Daniel	Gabbro (rock)
Danny	Quartz
Edward	Feather
Elliot	Coal
Emily	Sea Shell
Emma	Blue John (rock)
Jacob	Horse's Tooth
James	Moth
Joanne	Fossil
Kaylee	Amethyst
Kelly B	Rock
Kelly G	Leaf
Lavinia	Conkers
Lee	Woodlice
Lizzie	Peacock's Feather
Max	Tree Bark
Michael	Seahorse
Natalia	Pine Cone
Pagen	Flint
Rebecca	Fossil
Richard	Wasps' Nest
Robert	Volcanic Rock
Samantha B	Teasel
Samantha I	Geode (rock)
Samuel	Sandstone
Scott	Stone

APPENDIX B

THE ADULTS

The adults who were present throughout the two days were:

Julia Barnes who has worked as a learning support assistant at Wimbotsham School since 1997 and prior to that was organiser of the pre-school playgroup which meets at the school; her two children both attend the school.

Tony Brown who retired from primary headship in 1996 having taught in primary schools in Kent, Lincolnshire and Norfolk.

Annette Eggett who retired from primary headship in 1998 having taught in primary schools in Kent, London, Belfast and Norfolk.

Michael Foot who retired from primary headship in 1995 having taught in primary schools in Gloucestershire, Buckinghamshire and Norfolk.

Wendy Foot, class teacher, who had been headteacher of Wimbotsham School since 1991; she previously taught in primary schools in London, Gloucestershire, Buckinghamshire, Cambridgeshire and Norfolk.

Peter Holt who retired in 1992 having taught in secondary schools in Buckinghamshire, Somerset, Oxfordshire and Hertfordshire, and then having been an Education Officer and a Senior County Adviser in Norfolk.

THE LETTER

Walpole St Peter

2nd November 1998

Dear

I hope that you had a good half-term holiday.

I am delighted to say that Mr Holt, Mr Brown and I will be returning to your school to work with your class next Tuesday and Wednesday, 10th and 11th November. And we shall be bringing a friend of ours with us, Mrs Eggett, who until last Easter was the head teacher of Tilney All Saints School and who went with us to Runcton Holme and Magdalen Schools last term for their Poetry Week.

When we come this time, as well as doing some poetry writing, we will also be doing some art work. (I hear that you worked with a real live artist earlier this term!) And then each of you will be making a book in which you can put your work.

We would like you, please, to choose and bring to school one natural object which you will study. It has to be natural, not man-made. It may, for example, be a feather, stone, piece of rock, leaf, piece of wood, piece of tree bark, grass, berry, blossom, stem...

As well as poetry and art work, we would like you to do some research about your chosen object. So, in addition to using your school library, you might want to bring a book(s) from home or from the public library which might be helpful.

We all look forward to being with you again next Tuesday and Wednesday, and to seeing the exciting work that you produce.

Yours sincerely,

(M. W. Foot)

THE NORWEGIAN CORE CURRICULUM

We have quoted extensively from the *'Core Curriculum for Primary, Secondary and Adult Education in Norway'*, 1994.

It is an inspirational document – in its presentation, in its language and in its message – in a way that our own national curriculum documentation is not. It celebrates learners and learning in a way which is far removed from the relative sterility which characterises so much of our country's documentation.

We commend it to everyone who has an interest in education in this country, especially those policy-makers who perhaps do not realise, or will not admit, that there is another – and a better – way.

Another – and a better – view of learning than that which leads to the DfEE publishing guidelines which include, apparently without irony:

> *"The survey of pupils in the case study schools found that most pupils accepted <u>and even enjoyed homework</u>." (Our underlining.)*
> *('Homework: Guidelines for Primary and Secondary Schools', Department for Education and Employment, published and sent to all primary and secondary schools in England, November 1998)*

Another – and a better – way which values learning as a means of personal empowerment and fulfilment and which values learners as unique beings all at different stages on their journeys towards greater personal empowerment and fulfilment.

Norway's Core Curriculum document is published by the Royal Ministry of Church, Education and Research. It can be ordered through:

> Akademika als,
> Box 8134 Dep 0033 Oslo,
> NORWAY.

APPENDIX E (see Chapter 5, *'The Child'*)

JOANNE THE POET; JOANNE THE INSPIRATION FOR OTHERS

THE TREES I'N'T GRISTLING

'The trees i'n't gristling in the wind';
still they point out and up, outlined

against the vast unsullied blue.
Gymnastic branches contort, new

seasons waiting encased within
their tangled network. Each bent limb

drifts away unseen, absorbed by
cloaking space, branch lines fade to die.

At quiet night we marvelled in
reverent calm, and learned and wondered,

united in primeval rite.
With silence piercing far inside

our fragile beings, we kept safe
within our trees' towering embrace.

(Holt Hall, Norfolk)

EDUCATION NOW PUBLICATIONS

News and Review: quarterly publication promoting *Education Now's* vision

Information Packs: on *Home-based Education*, and on *Flexi-time Schooling*

Books: **The Caring Classroom** by Henry Pluckrose £9-95
Can classrooms be rescued from the dulling effetcs of rules, routines, regimentation?

Teaching Tomorrow: personal tuition as an alternative to school
by John Adcock, paperback £9-95 hardback £19-95
Offers a viable alternative to our 130-year-old centralised school-based system

Getting Started in Home Education: a Handbook
by Mary Ann Rose and Paul Stanbrook, £17-50
Written to help established and new families opting for home-based education.

Voices for Democracy: a North-South dialogue on education
for sustainable democracy edited by Clive Harber £11-95
The theme is education and democracy in Britain, Botswana, Namibi, & South Africa.

An Introduction to Curriculum for 3 to 5 Year-Olds by Viv Moriarty and
Iram Siraj-Blatchford £10-95
An excellent text for both experienced and new practitioners.

Developing Democratic Education edited by Clive Harber £9-95
Democracy is not genetic - it is learned behaviour, but schools are currently organised on anti-democratic principles.

Early Childhood Education: The Way Forward
edited by Philip Gammage and Janet Meighan £9-95
This is essential reading for all involved in the education of young children.

Learning Technology, Science and Social Justice: an integrated approach for 3-13 year
olds by John Siraj-Blatchford £13-95
In or out of school this book is full of practical suggestions.

Beyond Authoritarian School Management by Lynn Davies £9-95
How to move beyond the limitations of authoritarian school management.

Learning From Home-based Education edited by Roland Meighan £4-95
...the rich diversity of the home-based phenomenon is demonstrated.

Can You Teach Creativity? by Anna Craft et.al. £11-95
We need a new approach for fostering creativity and vision in education.

Praxis Makes Perfect: Critical Educational Research for Social Justice
by Iram Siraj-Blatchford £6-95

Full list from:
Education Now, 113 Arundel Drive, Bramcote Hills, Nottingham NG9 3FQ
Tel/fax 0115 925 7261 www.gn.apc.org/educationnow

EDUCATION NOW

Aim: *Education Now* is a UK-based organisation that is concerned to help develop arrangements for learning that will be humane, personalised and flexible enough to provide **'alternatives for everybody, all the time'**. It supports individuals and initiatives that try to make the best out of the present system in UK as we work for a better learning system to replace the present counter-productive, inhumane, anti-democratic one.

Justification: The present education system, based on a factory model of mass schooling, is now coming to be seen as more and more obsolete. In a rapidly changing world, with its information-rich environment and new communication technologies, and its new research on how the brain works, the case for traditional schooling gets weaker by the year. By contrast, the case for an education that will give people resourcefulness, flexibility, confidence in learning lifelong, readiness to unlearn redundant ideas, grows ever stronger.

Education Now seeks to foster new initiatives and developments in educational practice which actively involve learners in developing and defining their own curriculum in partnership with others. The present style of curriculum followed in the education system of this country, and in most of the world, does not recognise the crucial importance of democratic participative learning. The current persistence with a predominately authoritarian approach is:

- consigning our children to the obsolescence of a rigid mind-set.
- wasting the talents of many people
- damaging the self-confidence of many young people
- creating a dangerous cohort of frustrated and alienated youth

Those associated with *Education Now* share a commitment to the values which are set out in its *Statement of Purpose*. All the activities of the organisation are designed to promote the key ideas of flexibility, diversity, co-operation, democracy, self-motivation, learner-choice and responsibility, equal opportunity and personalisation of learning both in and out of state-provided education.

* * * * *

Status: Education Now Ltd is a research, writing, consultancy and publishing group, working as a co-operative. It is a non-government organisation. It is a company limited by guarantee, is registered for VAT, and is authorised to use a charity number, as a not-for-profit organisation.

Enquiries to: **Education Now,**
113 Arundel Drive, Bramcote Hills, Nottingham NG9 3FQ
Tel/fax 0115 925 7261

From the 'Statement of Purpose'

The vision of *EDUCATION NOW* includes:

- a focus on the uniqueness of individuals, of their learning experiences and of their many and varied learning styles

- support of education in human scale settings, including home-based education, small schools, mini-schools, and schools-within-schools, flexischooling and flexi-colleges

- recognition that learners themselves have the ability to make both rational and intuitive choices about their education

- advocacy of co-operative and democratic organisation of places of learning

- belief in the need to share national resources fairly, so that everyone has a real choice in education

- acceptance of Einstein's proposal that *imagination is more important than knowledge* in our modern and constantly changing world

- adoption of the Universal Declaration of Human Rights in general and the European Convention for the Protection of Human Rights and Fundamental Freedoms in particular, as a recognition of the limitations on choice in education.

EDUCATION NOW maintains that people learn best:

- when they are self-motivated

- when they take responsibility for their own lives and learning

- when they feel comfortable in their surroundings

- when teachers and learners value, trust, respect and listen to each other

- when education is seen as a life-long process